Angel Children

Those Who Die Before Accountability

Mary V. Hill

ISBN 13: 978-0-88290-017-9

Published by Horizon Publishers, an imprint of Cedar Fort, Inc.
 2373 W. 700 S., Springville, UT, 84663
Distributed by Cedar Fort, Inc., www.cedarfort.com

Cover design by Angela D. Olsen
Cover design © 2009 by Lyle Mortimer

Printed in the United States of America

10 9 8 7 6 5 4 3 2 1

Printed on acid-free paper

To the memory
of
Stephen Davis Hill
May 4 - August 14, 1971
"The crown without the conflict."

Shortly before Stephen died, my mother found this inscription on a child's tombstone in the Old Stone Church graveyard, Fairfield Township, Cumberland County, New Jersey. The inscription reads:

Annie
Daughter of Geo. Lorenzo
and Susan K. Elmer
Aged 3 years 4 months
and 15 days
The crown without the conflict.

Annie is my second cousin twice removed, and apparently lived in the 1870's. It is evident that the light of truth penetrated through false traditions for George and Susan Elmer, though they did not have a knowledge of the restoration. We selected the same inscription for little Stephen's stone. At the time of his passing, I was impressed that he was called to labor with our ancestors in the spirit world who did not know the fullness of the gospel while in mortality. For me, this inscription is a symbol of the bridge being built by Stephen as he labors in the spirit world and by me as I submit names of these dear people to the temples.

ACKNOWLEDGMENTS

It is a special privilege to express my gratitude in print to several people who have had a significant influence upon this book. My parents, Dr. Bruno and Mary Erety Elmer Vassel and my brother and sister, Bruno Vassel III and Elisabeth Vassel Andersen, have each contributed much both in the way of encouragement and in actual editing of the manuscript. They are wonderful people, with excellent thoughts.

Aaron and Bonnie Card, whose spiritual insights have had a profound influence upon my life, often guided my understanding as we faced the difficult experience of having Stephen come and then leave us.

William Grant Bangerter, formerly my mission president, has a penetrating understanding concerning the facing of trials and his counsel also has been sincerely appreciated. My lovely friends Melanie Empey Thygerson and Jeanne Redd Anthony each know better than words can express how dear to my heart they have been in my times of need. I thank them for the many hours they have spent discussing with me the contents of this work. However, I take full personal responsibility for the interpretations made within these pages.

Steve and Kaye Hendrickson Simpson also have done much to encourage me, and the use of their typewriter, when ours broke at a crucial time, was greatly appreciated.

The direction of this book was in large measure suggested by George Bickerstaff, and his counsel and editing were most helpful.

I am very grateful also to Duane Crowther whose insights and help as editor and publisher have been invaluable.

To my husband, Keith, I express my deepest gratitude and love. Words are unable to convey all that he has done. His advice has been excellent, and he has sacrificed many times to allow me the time to compile these teachings and thoughts, as have our children Keith, Jr., Lewis, Marety, Bruno and Christian.

CONTENTS

PREFACE

For three months and ten days our fifth child, Stephen, dwelt here with us in mortality. Then he was taken from us into the spirit world. What a precious fourteen weeks those were! At first came disbelief, tears, anguish; later answers to prayers, the submission of self-will, the closeness of the Savior.

When my husband and I realized that Stephen had a very serious congenital heart defect, we knew only in a general way the teachings of the prophets concerning little children who die, and also those teachings concerning retarded children which are closely related. But as we searched the scriptures and discourses of Church leaders, talked with wonderful friends, and prayed as we had never prayed before, gradually turmoil was replaced by peace, and then came an understanding of the revealed promise that: "ye shall know the truth, and the truth shall make you free." (John 8:32.) It is my sincere prayer that these truths will do the same for others.

—Mary Vassel Hill

CHAPTER 1

THE REALIZATION COMES SLOWLY

Stephen's Birth—Hope and Joy

One of the choicest times in life is immediately following the birth of a child. The hour of travail is past and the promise of new life has been fulfilled. All seems right with the world. So it was with the birth of our fifth child, Stephen. We did not dream, then, that for this child there was an eternal plan quite different from that of our others.

First Intimations of a Problem

When our pediatrician first mentioned a heart murmur, he also reassured us that heart murmurs in newborns are most often of minor significance. When Stephen was brought to me, I forgot all else in the warmth of the precious bundle I cuddled securely in my arms. Later, I uttered a silent prayer that the heart murmur would go away, and then began planning for the umpteenth time how we would rearrange the beds at home once Stephen outgrew his bassinet. We never did have to rearrange the beds.

When the doctor came in the next morning and said Stephen's heart murmur was definitely louder and that he'd be having an X-ray to see if his heart was enlarged, somehow I was totally unprepared. I hadn't really allowed myself to believe there could be anything wrong. I thanked him, and he said he'd let me know the results the following day. Tears, frustration, anguish, and even anger welled up in me, and I felt a helplessness I'd never known before. I prayed, "Father, Thy will be done, but can this be Thy will?" I had an overwhelming desire to cry, but felt I was not accepting the teachings of the gospel if I did. The tearing inside me was of an intensity I'd never dreamed possible.

Relentless Questions

My husband and a dear friend administered to Stephen before the X-ray, and many kind people telephoned and offered their prayers and reassurances. Questions pounded through my mind in an endless cycle. "Whose fault was this heart defect? My husband's and mine, for something we'd done or neglected to do? Or was it Stephen's, as a punishment for some premortal act? Or had Heavenly Father (impossible thought!) in some way made a mistake?" Questions— relentless, needing answers.

Thus the sometimes terrible, sometimes overwhelming, oftimes beautiful growth process began. Each parent who passes through the trial of having a special child faces a similar moment of realization—of truth, when the veil of security is rent and the fact that all is not well must be faced. In the few months before Stephen was taken, and in the many months since, I have run the full gamut of emotion as I have sought for understanding and the ability to accept. Why do some children develop an illness? Why are some in accidents, or born retarded, or with a fatal defect which snatches them early from their parents who want and love them? Those early days of realization are a period of deep introspection for the parents, an experience whose heights and depths can be appreciated only by those who actually face such a trial.

"Why me?" is the first, insistent question. Then, as the selfish thought submerges, the mind inquires in wiser tones. What of this little one's eternal future? Without a normal mortal existence, will he be forever handicapped? Or has a wise and merciful Father made provision for these little ones to reach the heights, just as He has for the rest of His spirit children? If so, how can they attain them?

Seeking to Understand through Faith

Although we do not know all the reasons why these things sometimes happen, through the revealed word of the scriptures, the teachings of Church leaders, and the experiences of others we may be uplifted and strengthened to be able to face these trials of life. In the words of Dr. Norman Vincent Peale: "People gain great victory over sorrow by means of their faith."[1]

---

1. Norman Vincent Peale, *Not Death At All* (New York: Prentice-Hall, Inc., 1948), p. 2.

CHAPTER 2

FACING THE CHALLENGE —A STRUGGLE

The Problem Develops

The pediatrician came into my room the following morning, all smiles, and told me that the X-rays did not show any enlargement of the heart. I held little Stephen very close and wept with relief and joy. After a few days, we went home to Daddy and four fascinated brothers and sisters. My husband Keith took pictures, and each child had a turn holding the tiny wonder.

As we left the hospital, the doctor asked me to bring Stephen into his office in about ten days, just to check the heart murmur again. I filed the instructions away in the back of my mind, and when the ten days had passed I said to my mother, "Oh, Stephen's doing so well. Maybe it's silly to go all the way over there today." But she with her quiet, gentle wisdom said that probably it would be best if we did.

When the pediatrician said the heart murmur was louder, and that he'd like to take an EKG (electrocardiogram), I again found myself in turmoil. The doctor telephoned with the results after several very anxious days. "Stephen's EKG appears to be within a normal range," he explained, "and so we'll just keep an eye on him. Call me if there is any problem." Again, a flood of relief. Not with the same confidence and intensity as the first time, after the X-ray, but still, a real relief.

In the weeks that followed, Stephen gained weight very slowly, and sometimes would turn extremely pale and cry especially hard. Upon recommendation, we decided to take him to a specialist in children's heart problems. Gradually, we began to realize that Stephen's heart murmur was not just a functional murmur without significance, but was representative of a much deeper problem.

Why Did This Happen, and Who Is To Blame?

During these weeks, again and again I wondered why this had happened to Stephen and to us. The idea that some arbitrary fate brings problems and difficulties into our lives is not consistent with the gospel. But by what forces are such things controlled?

One evening I knelt in prayer and expressed to Heavenly Father my questions, and asked Him to please tell me why Stephen had a congenital heart defect. The words came into my mind, formed in a complete sentence and indelible in their exactness. "You and Keith and Stephen and Heavenly Father covenanted in the pre-existence that Stephen would come to you under these conditions." No rationale, conceived in the mind of man, could possibly bring the peace that that sentence has brought. No one was guilty of error concerning Stephen. This problem was part of a plan, and even though the veil between the mortal life and the pre-mortal prevented us from knowing all the reasons why, we could rest assured that if we could really see the whole picture, we would not consider this a mistake in any way. In fact, we had all agreed to it long ago in heavenly realms.

This insight was given to me for our situation alone, and I do not share it as doctrine for the Church. For a further understanding of this question, consider the following. In the book of John, the Savior taught that a birth defect came neither from the sin of the child nor from the sins of the parents.

> And as Jesus passed by, he saw a man which was blind from his birth.
> And his disciples asked him, saying, Master, who did sin, this man, or his parents, that he was born blind?
> Jesus answered, Neither hath this man sinned, nor his parents: but that the works of God should be made manifest in him.[1]

James E. Talmage, commenting on this scripture, suggests the following:

> We are expressly told that he [the blind beggar] was born blind. That he might have been a sufferer from the sins of his parents was conceivable. The disciples evidently had been taught the great truth of an antemortal existence. It is further to be seen that they looked upon bodily affliction as the result of personal sin. Their generalization was too broad; for, while. . . [it is true that] individual wickedness may and does bring physical ills in its train, man is liable to err in his judgment as to the ultimate cause of affliction. The Lord's reply was sufficing; the man's blindness would be turned to account in bringing about a manifestation of divine power.[2]

This truth was also beautifully expressed in an editorial in the *Liahona:*

> The Prophet Joseph Smith once forbade the elders to teach that affliction in the form of sickness and death is always a punishment for sin. Our Heavenly Father will most willingly forgive the past if the law is obeyed in future. But in the hour of trial it is always a comfort to know that we have kept the commandments of the Lord as well as we could.[3]

---

1. John 9:1-3.

2. James E. Talmage, *Jesus the Christ* (Salt Lake City: Deseret Book Co., 1962), p. 413.

3. [Samuel O. Bennion?], "Why Do Little Children Die?", *Liahona—the Elder's Journal,* VI, No. 51 (June 5, 1909), 1229.

The reasons why trials such as these come into our lives are probably as varied and as personal as the people involved. An all-wise Father does know these individual reasons and has promised that as we seek, we shall find. In the words of Melvin J. Ballard:

> We cannot always understand the plans of the Almighty, but I feel sure that He does all things well and that sometimes the thing that seems almost like a disaster is a blessing in disguise. The only thing that matters is that we keep the right attitude. It is only when we become bitter that we let it change our whole lives, but when we can keep our courage and keep our eyes upon the mark and still go on toward our destiny, that is what matters. All these trials become purifying influences in our lives and leave us purer gold by and by.[4]

Effective Prayer—A Way to Answers

During the weeks when the doctors were still determining the exact nature of Stephen's heart condition, and why he had not gained weight well, I felt a real obligation as his mother to provide for him the best possible food. I was nursing him, and although the doctors kept reassuring me that his lack of weight gain was not due to nursing, still I wondered and worried. Should I add to his diet some other food, and if so, what? Would he be allergic to it and thus have more problems than he already had? Would it be better to stop nursing him altogether and put him onto a formula? Around and around in circles I thought and worried.

One evening I was talking on the phone to a lovely friend about Stephen and what to feed him, and she said to me, "Mary, have you prayed about it?" I had mentioned the problem briefly in my daily prayers, but a brief sentence about

---

4. Melvin R. Ballard, (comp.), Melvin J. Ballard . . . *Crusader for Righteousness* (Salt Lake City: Bookcraft, Inc., 1967), p. 275.

a problem wedged in between many other thoughts does not always bring answers as effectively as does prayer directed specifically to a certain problem. So, I knelt down in a private corner and earnestly talked to the Lord about what Stephen should be fed. I told Him Stephen's whole story, even though I knew He was already well aware of it. Then I told Heavenly Father about the specific area in which I needed help, explaining all the various possibilities I had thought of. First I said, "Shall I stop nursing him and switch to a formula?" Then I waited, but felt nothing. Next I said, "Shall I continue, then, to just nurse him without any other food?" Again, I waited but felt nothing at all. Finally I said, "Shall I continue to nurse him but also give him a high-protein, high-nutrition supplement once or twice a day?" Then I was filled with the sweet warmth of the Spirit. What a relief to know what would be best for precious Stephen! I poured over my family nutrition books and figured out a super-supplement which I gave him twice a day, and from then on he gained weight steadily.

Sometimes we are too brief with Heavenly Father. Oliver Cowdery was told as much by the Lord when He said:

> Behold, you have not understood; you have supposed that I would give it unto you, when you took no thought save it was to ask me.
>
> But, behold, I say unto you, that you must study it out in your mind; then you must ask me if it be right, and if it is right I will cause that your bosom shall burn within you; therefore, you shall feel that it is right.
>
> But if it is not right you shall have no such feelings, but you shall have a stupor of thought that shall cause you to forget the thing which is wrong.[5]

There are definite steps which, when followed, seem to be most helpful in really communicating with God and in

---

5. D&C 9:7-9.

receiving answers which are specific and solve daily problems. These are: (1) Talk to the Lord, telling Him the whole story as if He were not aware of any of the details, and then ask for His help in knowing what to do. (2) Brainstorm all possible solutions. Sometimes this requires hours and even days of thought as you go about the routine tasks of life, and sometimes it can be done on your knees. (3) Go back to Heavenly Father. Remind Him of the basic problem and tell Him each of your ideas. Sometimes you'll feel sweet peace and warmth as you explain your first idea and if you try to go on to the others you feel the Spirit leave and you know that's the answer. Sometimes you'll present to the Lord your various ideas and none will bring the peace of the Spirit. Then tell the Lord you've thought of all the solutions you could and you yield now to His divine will. At moments like this, many times a flash of insight will come, often in the form of a complete sentence, which is deeply imprinted upon your mind and which stays with you in exactly those words as time goes by. Of course, when one receives answers such as these, one is under an obligation to follow through and do as the Lord has directed. One may do so with the sure knowledge that there is no better way![6]

Accepting the Reality of the Situation

As time went on, the doctors told us it would be necessary for Stephen to have open heart surgery, and in the weeks prior to the operation I often wept and said I wished I could take his place. One evening we had some choice friends to dinner, and I expressed these sentiments to them. One of the sisters who

---

6. See also George J. Romney, (comp.), *Look To God and Live: Discourses of Marion G. Romney* (Salt Lake City: Deseret Book Co., 1971), pp. 64-72.

had also had a child with a very serious problem said to me, "You must face the reality of the situation. Heavenly Father did not want you to do this, but Stephen." How that thought helped me! Particularly during the thirty-six hours after the surgery, every time I'd look at him I'd say, "Face the reality, Mary. This was in Heavenly Father's hands, not yours." I wonder if likewise the Father would not have gladly stepped in and taken the Savior's place in Gethsemane and on the Cross, but that was not His role. He too had to face the reality of the situation. Elder Melvin J. Ballard, in discussing this very idea, said:

> He had the power to save and he loved his Son, and he would have saved him. . . . Oh, in the moment that he might have saved his Son, I thank him and praise him that he did not fail us, for he had love for us. I rejoice that he did not interfere, and that his love for us made it possible for him to endure to look upon the sufferings of his Son and give him finally to us, our Savior and our Redeemer.[7]

I am glad I did not have the power to make the choice the Father was required to make. But I can, in some small measure at least, appreciate what it is to see one's beloved son suffer so. Each parent who watches a child suffer must face the reality of the situation, and accept what is beyond his power to change. In the words of John Taylor, "It is necessary men should be tried and purged and purified and made perfect through suffering."[8]

---

7. Carl H. Jacob, *While of these Emblems* (Salt Lake City: Deseret Book Co., 1962), pp. 100-01.

8. Alma and Clea Burton, *For They Shall Be Comforted* (Salt Lake City: Deseret Book Co., 1970), p. 11.

Faith and Healing

One evening my husband mentioned to me that in connection with his work the following day, he'd be seeing Elder Richard L. Evans, of the Council of the Twelve, and asked if I would like to have Elder Evans administer to Stephen. I said I would, but I felt a deep responsibility not to ask the Lord for a blessing for Stephen that was not in accordance with His mind and will. Therefore, that evening after everyone was asleep, I prayed and asked the Lord concerning His will for our little son. The answer was two indelible sentences, which I realize now as I look back over the events that followed, were sublime in their wisdom. The sentences were, "It is not necessarily My will that Stephen come into the spirit world now. If he remains with you, it will be contingent upon your faith." Oh, the beauty of that answer! Had the Lord told me at that point that it was definitely His will that Stephen be taken in the near future, I'd have given up and resigned myself to the inevitable, thus losing a marvelous opportunity to learn and grow.

Elder Evans administered to Stephen the following day, and gave him a most beautiful blessing in which the need for faith was again pointed out. Thus I was guided to a fervent quest for greater understanding of faith and what constitutes faith to heal. I wanted to know what one needs to have faith in; faith in faith itself, or faith in one's own ability to develop strong faith, or faith in the priesthood, or in the men who hold the priesthood? How can one have faith and still say, "Thy will be done"? Is faith saying, "He will be all right because of my great faith"? My search led me to the following understanding.

Faith Centers in Christ

The scriptures teach us that when we exercise faith, it is not supposed to be faith in faith itself, or faith in one's own faith, but rather, faith in the Lord Jesus Christ. Note Alma's prayer in behalf of Zeezrom who was sick, "being very low with a burning fever":

> And then Alma cried unto the Lord, saying: O Lord our God, have mercy on this man, and heal him according *to his faith which is in Christ.*
> And when Alma had said these words, Zeezrom leaped upon his feet, and began to walk.[9]

Zeezrom's faith was centered in Christ, and thus the gift of healing was given. Sometimes, as in the case of a small or retarded child, this faith in the Savior must be exercised by those around him, as he himself is not capable of such understanding. This requires an attitude of complete submission of one's own, selfish will, and the exercising instead of an absolute trust in the wisdom and in the ability of the Savior to do what is best in each particular situation. One might say to oneself, "My child can be healed, by my faith in the Savior and His power to do it. But the final decision is up to Him." Thus we do not find ourselves in the situation of demanding, which is contrary to the ways of the Lord. This is a positive kind of submission—a realization that there is a Higher Being which is able to make a much wiser decision than is man with his limited understanding. Such an attitude is quite different from just giving up—characterized by hopelessness and a feeling of being overwhelmed by forces far beyond one's control.

---

9. Alma 15:10-11. Author's italics.

Faith and Priesthood Administration

In the Doctrine and Covenants, we are taught that "the elders of the church, two or more, shall be called, and shall pray for and lay their hands upon them in my name; and if they die they shall die unto me, and if they live they shall live unto me."[10]

Marvelous accounts of priesthood administrations which have led to the healing of the sick are available to Latter-day Saints, and many of us know of such incidents within our own families and wards or branches. However, there are also occasions when in spite of the administration of the priesthood, those who are sick do not get well. How then does this priesthood power work in our lives? This same question was asked by a mother in a letter to the *Liahona* in 1909. The editor replied:

> She is troubled to understand why her children were taken, notwithstanding the prayers that were offered up, and the authority of the priesthood that was invoked and exercised, in their behalf. While it is true that God has conferred upon mortal man the priesthood by which, within certain limitations, they have power to act in his name, it is not true that he has conferred upon them the keys of life and death. These keys are held in hands higher than those of mortals. They are used only with a proper regard for the past, the present, and the future; our condition in the spirit world before we came here, our condition here, and our condition in the world to come. Mortal men have not sufficient knowledge of all these conditions to use power over life and death wisely and justly; and therefore this power is, to a great extent, and always in the final issue, withheld from them. By the prayer of faith they can often influence the result, but the decision always rests with God.[11]

---

10. D&C 42:44.

11. [Bennion?], *Liahona—the Elder's Journal*, pp. 1227-28.

Elder Spencer W. Kimball, in his thought-provoking talk, *Tragedy or Destiny,* suggests to us:

> The power of the Priesthood is limitless but God has wisely placed upon each of us certain limitations. I may develop Priesthood power as I perfect my life. I am grateful that even through the Priesthood I cannot heal all the sick. I might heal people who should die, I might relieve people of suffering who should suffer. I fear I would frustrate the purposes of God.
>
> Would you dare to take the responsibility of bringing back to life your loved ones? I, myself, would hesitate to do so. I am grateful that we may always pray: "Thy will be done in all things, for Thou knowest what is best." I am glad I do not have the decisions to make. We might consign loved ones to loss of faculties, loss of powers, terrible doom.[12]

We must remember that priesthood administration is an ordinance, and that one is not healed by the ordinance, necessary though it is, but by faith in the source of priesthood power, which is Jesus Christ.

Joseph Smith, who healed hundreds of people during the course of his life, was not able to heal his own twin infants when they sickened and died. The Lord has purpose in whether or not one is healed.

Faith and a Time to Die

The scriptures indicate that there is more than mere chance involved in the length of one's life here in mortality. Consider for instance:

> To every thing there is a season, and a time to every purpose under the heaven:
> A time to be born, and a time to die;[13]

---

12. Spencer W. Kimball, *Tragedy or Destiny* (Provo, Utah: BYU Extension Publications, 1961), pp. 7-8.

13. Ecclesiastes 3:1-2.

And:

> Man that is born of a woman is of few days. . . .
>
> Seeing his days are determined, the number of his months are with thee, thou hast appointed his bounds that he cannot pass;[14]

As we exercise faith in the Savior, we will do so with greater understanding if we keep in mind His words: "And again, it shall come to pass that he that hath faith in me to be healed, and is not appointed unto death, shall be healed."[15]

Perhaps an allegory will help us to better understand some phases of this subject:

> In a certain home in a stake of Zion a little child lay very ill. Other children of that household had died. The angel of death stood by the bedside. The father was a good man of great faith, and he called in elders who were likewise good men of strong faith. The ordinance of the Lord's house for healing the sick was administered, and prayers of faith ascended on high. The death angel hesitated, and another angel, whose errand was life, entered the home. The two personages from the other world conversed. "I came to take this child," said the death angel. "I heard the prayer of faith and am come to consider the matter," said the other angel. They were undecided and, obedient to law, they left the home of the sick child and laid the case before an angel of higher authority. He heard what both had to say and answered: "The child is wanted in heaven; let the angel of death bring it hither."
>
> The angel of death returned to the child's home. Again the father prayed in mighty faith, and again did his brethren join him with all their faith, which was great. The angel of death again hesitated, and the same messenger of life who met him there before, came again and said to him: "You know such prayers as these have weight with the Lord; we must consider

---

14. Job 14:1, 5.

15. D&C 42:48.

this case further." They went again before the higher angel to whom the angel of life told what mighty faith was being shown in the stricken child's behalf.

The higher angel looked grave. "We must give heed to the prayer of faith," he said. Then spoke the death angel: "There are those in heaven whose love for and claim upon the child are equal to the love and claim of its earthly parents, and they are pleading for it in faith." "We will lay the case before the Council," said the higher angel; "because of the faith exercised in it, and its importance, it must go for decision to higher authority."

In a palace in heaven whose beauty and splendor exceeded the powers of mortal man's imagination, the Council, a body of heavenly personages of great wisdom, mercy and authority, sat; and the three angels appeared before it. The higher angel explained why he had not decided the case. The death angel gave reasons why the child should be taken. The angel of life urged the prayers of faith which had been offered in the child's behalf, and other children of the same parents that had been taken. The president of the Council called for certain records, and they were produced. After a search of them he said: "The child's mission on earth is fulfilled. The claim of its earthly parents has been fully satisfied, and the rights of those in heaven who have a claim upon it must be conceded. Were not such the case the prayer of faith would surely keep it in the world. But as the case stands the child may come to heaven."

The angel of life pleaded: "But the parents will be crushed, and their faith in prayer and the goodness of God will be shattered." "Not so," replied the president of the Council, "for we will send the angel of comfort to their home, and the grace of God will be given to them, and in their grief shall they find new testimonies of the goodness and mercy of God. And it shall be shown to them that what they asked, even in faith, was asked amiss."

The angel of death went a third time to the home, and took the child. The heartstrings of the parents were torn, and for a season they would not be comforted. But after a time they remembered that their child had a Mother in heaven as well as on earth, and that the claims of those above are stronger than the claims of those below. They looked about them and saw the sin and suffering of this world. Selfishness lost its power in their hearts, the peace of the Holy Spirit came to them, and they rejoiced in the knowledge that their little ones who had been taken were saved in the kingdom of God through the atonement of Christ.[16]

As far as we are concerned, life on this earth is sacred and should be preserved as best we can. Therefore, when sickness or accident or a similar trial comes, we might pray to the Father saying, "Since Thou hast not revealed to me that Thou doest require this person at this time (that being the case after sincere prayer), I will do all I can to exercise full faith that this person can and will be healed by Thee. I know Thou hast the power, and as far as I can understand, there is no reason why he should not be healed. If, however, in Thy wisdom Thou hast reasons why he should not be healed, and we should not know in advance, I will accept Thy will with peace." By so doing we will not place ourselves in the position of setting our will against that of the Divine. In the words of Spencer W. Kimball:

> I am positive in my mind that the Lord has planned our destiny. We can shorten our lives but I think we cannot lengthen them very much. Sometime we'll understand fully, and when we see back from the vantage point of the future we shall be satisfied with many of the happenings of this life which seemed so difficult for us to comprehend.
>
> We knew before we were born that we were coming to the earth for bodies and experience and that we would have joys and sorrows, pain and comforts, ease and hardships, health and sickness, successes and disappointments, and we knew also that we would die. We accepted all these eventualities with a glad heart, eager to accept both the favorable and unfavorable. We

---

16. [Bennion?], *Liahona—the Elder's Journal*, pp. 1229-30.

were undoubtedly willing to have a mortal body even if it were deformed. We eagerly accepted the chance to come earthward even though it might be for a day, a year, or a century. Perhaps we were not so much concerned whether we should die of disease, of accident, or of senility. We were willing to come, and take life as it came and as we might organize and control it, and this without murmur, complaint or unreasonable demands. . . .[17]

Elder Melvin J. Ballard also said, concerning this matter:

If we could be conscious always of the prime purpose for which we are here it would be easier for us to reconcile ourselves to death. I remember going into a carpet factory where they were making beautiful rugs. I approached from the seamy side. The shuttle was flying back and forth and the warp and woof were being made but there was not any design there. It was all ravelings and ends. It was just like life. When I stepped around on the other side it was another picture. It was the same operation—the same things exactly, only this was the design side. The color was blending; the figure was developing. There was not any failure there.

We look at sorrows like death and we think they are tragedies, but we are only looking at things from the seamy side. There is another side to the picture, the designer's side—God's side. And there are no blunders there. Some day we will see it. Some day we will be able to say, "The Lord liveth! The Lord giveth and the Lord taketh away. Blessed be the name of the Lord!"[18]

Faith Sufficient to Heal Is a Gift

The night before Stephen's open-heart surgery, I felt a deep need for strength to face the next days and weeks. I went to the temple and sat in the celestial room and poured my soul out to Heavenly Father. I prayed and wept and said, "Father,

---

17. Kimball, *Tragedy or Destiny,* p. 12.
18. Ballard, *Crusader for Righteousness,* p. 276.

how can You say to me that whether or not Stephen stays with us is contingent upon my faith? How can You put his life in my hands? It's not fair!" Never in my life have I prayed in such anguish and turmoil, and yet felt the Spirit of the Lord so strongly. I had tried the best I knew to exercise faith, and we'd fasted, prayed, had him administered to and kept his name on the temple prayer list. But suppose we'd failed, and our faith would be judged insufficient? I felt as if I held his little life in my weak hands. In answer to my outpourings the words came to my mind clearly, "Faith to heal Stephen is a gift." Thus the Lord assured me that no matter how hard we tried to have faith, He would make the final decision as to whether or not the Divine power necessary to heal Stephen, which power is controlled by the law of faith, would be given. The weight that was lifted from my shoulders was inexpressible. I was filled with sweet peace as I yielded my will to the will of the Savior, and put Stephen and myself in His hands.

Since then, I have learned that the words whispered to my soul there in the temple are also taught us in the scriptures. In the 46th section of the Doctrine and Covenants the Lord, speaking of the gifts which are given unto the church says, "For all have not every gift given unto them; . . ."[19] and then He goes on to say: "And again, to some it is given to have faith to be healed, And to others it is given to have faith to heal."[20] It appears that although this gift may be given sometimes in our lives—for I know that it has been in the past in mine—on other occasions if a person is "appointed unto death"[21] the gift is withheld. Such was the case with our precious Stephen.

---

19. D&C 46:11.
20. D&C 46:19-20.
21. D&C 42:48.

Just as one repents to the best of one's ability, but then salvation comes as a gift,[22] likewise one must exercise faith in the Savior to the best of one's ability, but realize that the final giving or not giving of sufficient faith to be healed is a decision which must remain with the Lord. In the words of J. Reuben Clark:

> As I think about faith, this principle of power, I am obliged to believe that it is an intelligent force. Of what kind, I do not know. But it is superior to and overrules all other forces of which we know. It is the principle, the force, by which the dead are restored to life.
>
> I do not believe that the Lord, that God permits any man to have faith that would overrule his purposes. In that connection, I call to your attention the fact that the Savior himself plead that his crucifixion might be turned aside. Yet, on one occasion he said, when he asked that the hour might be passed on, ". . . but for this cause came I unto this hour." (John 12:27.) The Son of God was not given the necessary faith at the time to enable him to turn aside the purposes reached by himself and the Father before. . . .[23]

Stephen's Passing

The following fifty-six hours after my prayer in the temple were an experience of wordless agony for Stephen, for Keith and for me. After five hours of surgery the doctors were quite encouraged. Keith and I stayed by our sweet son's side day and night as he struggled for his life, but he had a more and more difficult time as various complications set in. On the evening of the second day, feeling the need for sustaining comfort, Keith and I went into a side room at the hospital and

---

22. D&C 6:13.

23. Roy W. Doxey, *The Latter-day Prophets and The Doctrine and Covenants* (Salt Lake City: Deseret Book Co., 1963), p. 91.

knelt together. We were filled with the most overwhelmingly peaceful spirit, as Keith told the Lord how we would love to have little Stephen in our family circle, but we would accept His will. If Stephen was to die, he asked that the Lord please take him soon. We felt impressed to tell our little son goodbye, so we went into the Intensive Care unit and each caressed him and whispered our farewells. I could literally feel myself place Stephen in one arm of the Savior and myself in the other as I laid down to sleep there at the hospital, and with the transfer of my burden to Him, I slept peacefully through the night.

We awoke at 5:00 a.m. and went into the Intensive Care unit and saw Stephen again. At 5:55 a.m. the doctor came out and told us he was gone.

CHAPTER 3

BEYOND THE GRAVE

As the first rays of morning light burst over the peaks of the Wasatch Range, I wrapped our little son in a receiving blanket and sat and rocked and loved him. For a beautiful hour and a half I held him there. It was so peaceful, and yet—how clear it was that dear Stephen's spirit had left his mortal tabernacle and now I held in my arms only the little house I had helped to create for him. He had left as quietly as he'd come, gone on to other spheres—"the crown without the conflict." Finally I gently laid him on his bed, never to hold him again in this mortal world.

But already in my heart I was inquiring about Stephen's other half—his shining eyes and dancing smile! Where was he and what was he doing? Would his body ever develop into adult size? Would I hold him and love him and nurture him at some future date? These and similar questions filled my mind. How grateful I have been for the beautiful truths of the restored Gospel of Jesus Christ, as I have learned more and more about what the Lord has planned for little ones who die before becoming accountable. It is a great blessing to live at a time when such knowledge is available to those who mourn the loss of a child!

A False Concept
Regarding the Death of Children

Imagine the feelings of the mother described in the following experience by Joseph Fielding Smith:

Well do I remember the anguish in the heart of an earnest, loving mother who was told by a well-meaning but misguided priest that her dead infant was eternally lost because the child had not been christened.

I was visiting at the home of this mother, and she related the following story. Several years before, she had lost a little child. He had not been taken to the minister for sprinkling and had, in that condition, died. The parents sought their minister and asked him to conduct the funeral and give their little one Christian burial; however, this humble request was solemnly, but nonetheless brutally, denied. The parents were told the child was forever lost. Heartbroken, they laid their little child away as an outcast might have been buried, without the rites of that church and without "Christian burial." How the hearts of those fond parents ached; how their feelings were torn asunder!

For several years this mother, with faith in the teachings of that priest, suffered the most acute mental agony. She knew it was not the fault of her infant that he had not been christened. He was innocent of any wrong. Was not that wrong her own? And in her mind, because of this false teaching, was not she responsible for the eternal suffering of this little one? She felt as a repentant murderer who could not restore the life he had taken, and in this anguish of soul she suffered the punishment of the damned.

It was a happy day when I came to the home of this tormented mother. Even now I can see the joy that came into her tormented face when I explained to her that this doctrine was false—as false as the depths of hell whence it came. I taught her this was not the doctrine of Jesus Christ, who loved little · children and who declared that they belonged to the kingdom of heaven.[1]

Words cannot begin to tell the weight of the burden one must carry when facing the death of one's child. However, the load is greatly lightened when our thoughts and hopes are

---

1. Joseph Fielding Smith, "Justice for the Dead," *The Ensign,* II, No. 3 (March, 1972), 4.

centered upon those eternal truths which change the face of death from a horrible and overwhelming monster into a shining crack in a door, behind which one catches a glimpse of eternal exaltation.

Purity of Little Children

Over the centuries, a false religious doctrine has developed among Christian churches in which it is believed that because Adam and Eve sinned long ago in the Garden of Eden, little children are born under the curse of original sin—cast out of God's presence eternally unless they are christened.

The Lord has revealed through a modern prophet that this doctrine is false. In the *Pearl of Great Price* He says:

> The Son of God hath atoned for original guilt, wherein the sins of the parents cannot be answered upon the heads of the children, for they are whole from the foundation of the world.[2]

And in the *Doctrine and Covenants* we read: "And God having redeemed man from the fall, men became again, in their infant state, innocent before God."[3] Thus we are assured that in Christ, even without christening, ". . . the infant perisheth not that dieth in his infancy,"[4] and "little children also have eternal life."[5]

Little Children Need No Baptism

How grateful this mother must have felt when Joseph Fielding Smith recounted to her the words of Mormon,

---

2. Moses 6:54.

3. D&C 93:38.

4. Mosiah 3:18.

5. Mosiah 15:25.

concerning the baptism of little children, found in the *Book of Mormon:*

> And after this manner did the Holy Ghost manifest the word of God unto me; wherefore, my beloved son, I know that it is solemn mockery before God, that ye should baptize little children. . . .
>
> Little children need no repentance, neither baptism. Behold, baptism is unto repentance to the fulfilling the commandments unto the remission of sins.
>
> But little children are alive in Christ, even from the foundation of the world; if not so, God is a partial God, and also a changeable God, and a respecter to persons; for how many little children have died without baptism!
>
> Wherefore, if little children could not be saved without baptism, these must have gone to an endless hell
>
> . . . wherefore, I love little children with a perfect love; and they are all alike and partakers of salvation.[6]

This mother learned that day that her little one, instead of being cast off, was in a most favored position.[7] Sidney Sperry comments concerning these little ones: "Most of us have observed the light and truth in little children of a tender age."[8]

Children Who Die Are Heirs of the Celestial Kingdom

Joseph Smith wrote: "And I also beheld that all children who die before they arrive at the years of accountability, are

---

6. Moroni 8:9, 11-13, 17.

7. See also Hyrum L. Andrus, *God, Man, and the Universe* (Salt Lake City: Book craft , Inc., 1968), pp. 432-37.

8. Sidney B. Sperry, *Doctrine and Covenants Compendium* (Salt Lake City: Bookcraft, Inc., 1960), p. 481.

saved in the celestial kingdom of heaven."[9] Children become accountable at the age of eight years,[10] and should they die before this age they return to their Father in Heaven and have salvation. This applies to all children. In the words of Joseph Fielding Smith: "The revelations of the Lord to the Prophet Joseph Smith declare that all little children who die are heirs of the celestial kingdom. This would mean the children of every race."[11]

Children Who Die Are Redeemed from the Temptations of Satan

A most interesting and thought-provoking result of the redemption of little children by the Savior is that "they cannot sin, for power is not given unto Satan to tempt little children, until they begin to become accountable. . ."[12] Joseph Fielding Smith gives us the following explanations in relation to this doctrine:

> Little children who die before the age of accountability are saved in the celestial kingdom. . . . Serious thinking would tell us that if these children are saved, they are not subject to a later trial by the temptation and buffeting of Satan. . . . Revelations given in our day also show that little children who are deprived of the experiences in mortal life are, by eternal decree, redeemed from the temptation of Satan.[13]

---

9. Joseph Smith, *History of the Church of Jesus Christ of Latter-day Saints,* ed. B. H. Roberts (7 vols.; Salt Lake City: Deseret Book Co., 1959), II, 381 (January 21, 1836). (Hereafter cited as HC.).

10. D&C 68:27.

11. Joseph Fielding Smith, *Doctrines of Salvation,* comp. Bruce R. McConkie (3 vols.; Salt Lake City: Bookcraft, Inc., 1967), II, 55.

12. D&C 29:47.

13. Joseph Fielding Smith, "Little Children in the Celestial Kingdom," *Improvement Era,* LIX (October, 1956), 702.

Satan will be loosed to gather his forces after the millennium. The people who will be tempted, will be people living on this earth, and they will have every opportunity to accept the gospel or reject it. Satan will have nothing to do whatever with little children, or grown people who have received their resurrection and entered into the celestial kingdom.

Satan cannot tempt little children in this life, nor in the spirit world, nor after their resurrection.[14]

In the words of Alvin R. Dyer:

Children who die as to natural death in their infancy, or before the age of accountability, are redeemed in the Lord. These are of the more noble spirits of the pre-existence, and because of their purity, will have the exceptional joy of having their tabernacles of flesh and bone mature and grow to the full stature of their spirit bodies under more favorable conditions of existence during the millennium.[15]

The condition of these children is similar to that of those who will be born during the millennium when "children shall grow up without sin unto salvation."[16] What a wonderful feeling it has given me to realize that Stephen has passed away without sin, and that Satan has no power over him.

The Prophet Joseph Smith, who lost four of his own children and one adopted child in the course of his life, expressed the following thoughts:

I have meditated upon the subject, and asked the question, why it is that infants, innocent children, are taken away from us, especially those that seem to be the most intelligent and interesting. The strongest reasons that present themselves to my

---

14. Smith, *Doctrines of Salvation,* II, 56-57.

15. Alvin Rulon Dyer, *Who Am I?* (Salt Lake City: Deseret Book Co., 1966), pp. 482-83.

16. D&C 45:58.

mind are these. . . . The Lord takes many away, even in infancy, that they may escape the envy of man, and the sorrows and evils of this present world; they were too pure, too lovely, to live on earth; therefore, if rightly considered, instead of mourning we have reason to rejoice as they are delivered from evil, and we shall soon have them again. . . .

The only difference between the old and the young dying is, one lives longer in heaven and eternal light and glory than the other, and is freed a little sooner from this miserable, wicked world. Not withstanding all this glory, we for a moment lose sight of it, and mourn the loss, but we do not mourn as those without hope.[17]

Life in the Spirit World

Having come to an understanding that Stephen is free from sin and beyond the power of Satan, more questions filled my heart. Where is Stephen now? What is he doing? What is that world like, and how far from us is it? What activities do those who are there participate in?

Many Church leaders have painted beautiful word-pictures of the life beyond this one for us which convey much understanding. In General Conference Elder Ezra Taft Benson said: "The spirit world is not far away. Sometimes the veil between this life and the life beyond becomes very thin. Our loved ones who have passed on are not far from us."[18] Brigham Young once asked, "But where is the spirit world?" He then answered his own question by saying:

It is here. . . . Do (spirits) go beyond the boundaries of this organized earth? No, they do not. They are brought forth

---

17. HC, IV, 553-54.

18. *Official Report of the Annual General Conference of the Church of Jesus Christ of Latter-day Saints* (Salt Lake City: The Church, 1971), p. 18 (April 3, 1971).

upon this earth, for the express purpose of inhabiting it to all eternity. . . .

If the Lord would permit it, and it was His will that it should be done, you could see the spirits that have departed from this world, as plainly as you now see bodies with your natural eyes.[19]

Brigham Young has also given us the following description of the world of spirits:

What will be the nature of our pursuits in a state of being in which we shall possess more vigor and a higher degree of intelligence than we possess here? Shall we have labor? Shall we have enjoyment in our labor? Shall we have any object of pursuit, or shall we sit and sing ourselves away to everlasting bliss? . . .

I would like to say to you, my friends and brethren, if we could see things as they are, and as we shall see and understand them, this dark shadow and valley is so trifling that we shall turn round and look upon it and think, when we have crossed it, why this is the greatest advantage of my whole existence, for I have passed from a state of sorrow, grief, mourning, woe, misery, pain, anguish and disappointment into a state of existence, where I can enjoy life to the fullest extent as far as that can be done without a body. My spirit is set free, I thirst no more, I want to sleep no more, I hunger no more, I tire no more, I run, I walk, I labor, I go, I come, I do this, I do that, whatever is required of me, nothing like pain or weariness. I am full of life, full of vigor, and I enjoy the presence of my heavenly Father, by the power of his Spirit.[20]

Much as we miss Stephen's presence in our family circle, I am grateful that he is free from the physical handicaps which, had

19. *Journal of Discourses* (26 vols.; Los Angeles: General Printing and Lithograph Co., 1961), III, 367-69 (June 22, 1856). (Hereafter cited as JD).

20. JD, XVII, 142.

he continued in mortality, would have caused him much pain and grief.

The Spirits of Children Who Die Are Adult in Stature

But what size is Stephen's spirit now? If it is the size his body was when he died, who will care for him? We read in *Doctrines of Salvation:* "When a baby dies, it goes back into the spirit world, and the spirit assumes its natural form as an adult, for we were all adults before we were born."[21] Joseph F. Smith reaffirms this doctrine and tells us of the most interesting account of Bishop Edward Hunter in the early days of the Church:

> The spirits of our children are immortal before they come to us, and their spirits, after bodily death, are like they were before they came. They are as they would have appeared if they had lived in the flesh, to grow to maturity, or to develop their physical bodies to the full stature of their spirits. If you see one of your children that has passed away, it may appear to you in the form in which you would recognize it, the form of childhood; but if it came to you as a messenger bearing some important truth, it would perhaps come as the spirit of Bishop Edward Hunter's son (who died when a little child) came to him, in the stature of full-grown manhood, and revealed himself to his father, and said: "I am your son."
>
> Bishop Hunter did not understand it. He went to my father and said: "Hyrum, what does that mean? I buried my son when he was only a little boy, but he has come to me a full-grown man—a noble, glorious, young man, and declared himself my son. What does it mean?"

---

21. Smith, *Doctrines of Salvation,* II, 56.

Father [Hyrum Smith, the Patriarch] told me that the Spirit of Jesus Christ was full-grown before He was born into the world; and so our children were full-grown and possessed their full stature in the spirit, before they entered mortality, the same stature that they will possess after they have passed away from mortality, and as they will also appear after the resurrection, when they shall have completed their mission.[22]

So, Stephen's spirit is the size he would have been had he grown to manhood. I am grateful I need have no worries as to his well-being, for I am sure he is able to care for himself. That is a great relief to me! Brigham Young also assures us that our little ones are not lonely, for he said:

We have more friends behind the veil than on this side, and they will hail us more joyfully than you were ever welcomed by your parents and friends in this world; and you will rejoice more when you meet them than you ever rejoiced to see a friend in this life; and then you shall go on from step to step, from rejoicing to rejoicing, and from one intelligence and power to another, our happiness becoming more and more exquisite and sensible as we proceed in the words and powers of life.[23]

President Jedediah M. Grant passed away while he was first counselor to Brigham Young. During the last two days of his life his spirit went into the spirit world several times and then returned to mortality. He told his friend, Heber C. Kimball, of his experiences and later at President Grant's funeral Brother Kimball gave the following account:

He said to me, brother Heber, I have been into the spirit world two nights in succession, and, of all the dreads that ever came across me, the worst was to have to again return to my body, though I had to do it. But O, says he, the order and

---

22. Joseph F. Smith, *Gospel Doctrine* (Salt Lake City: Deseret Book Co., 1963), p. 455.

23. JD, VI, 349.

government that were there! When in the spirit world, I saw the order of righteous men and women; beheld them organized in their several grades, and there appeared to be no obstruction to my vision; I could see every man and woman in their grade and order. I looked to see whether there was any disorder there, but there was none; neither could I see any death nor any darkness, disorder or confusion. He said that the people he there saw were organized in family capacities, and when he looked at them he saw grade after grade, and all were organized and in perfect harmony. He would mention one item after another and say, "Why, it is just as brother Brigham says it is; it is just as he told us many a time." . . .

He saw the righteous gathered together in the spirit world, and there were no wicked spirits among them. He saw his wife; she was the first person that came to him. He saw many that he knew, but did not have conversation with any except his wife Caroline. She came to him. and he said that she looked beautiful and had their little child, that died on the Plains, in her arms, and said, "Mr. Grant, here is little Margaret; you know that the wolves ate her up, but it did not hurt her; here she is all right. . . ."[24] "To my astonishment," he said, "when I looked at families there was a deficiency in some, there was a lack, for I saw families that would not be permitted to come and dwell together, because they had not honored their calling here." . . .

He also spoke of the buildings he saw there, remarking that the Lord gave Solomon wisdom and poured gold and silver into his hands that he might display his skill and ability, and said that the temple erected by Solomon was much inferior to the most ordinary buildings he saw in the spirit world.

---

24. See pages 41-42 concerning seeing a child in the spirit world as a child rather than as a full-grown spirit.

25. JD, IV, 135-36.

In regard to gardens, says brother Grant, "I have seen good gardens on this earth, but I never saw any to compare with those that were there. I saw flowers of numerous kinds, and some with from fifty to a hundred different colored flowers growing upon one stalk.[25]

The Great Work in the Spirit World Is Preaching the Gospel

What might Stephen be doing in the spirit world? Because his spirit is adult in size, with the adult mentality he possessed prior to his mortal birth, he would be able to actively participate in the work that goes on there. Alvin R. Dyer tells us:

> The spirit world, while a place of rest and comfort to the righteous, is not a place of "do nothing bliss." It is a place of activity and action. There are apostles, prophets, elders and members of the Church of the Saints, holding keys of the priesthood and power to teach, comfort, instruct and proclaim the gospel to their fellow spirits. The righteous spirits gather together to prepare and qualify themselves for a future day.[26]

"The great work in the world of spirits is the preaching of the gospel to those who are imprisoned by sin and false traditions."[27] It gives me great joy to think that perhaps Stephen is engaged in this great labor and might even be preaching to those of our ancestors who did not have the opportunity of hearing the gospel while living in mortality. Duane S. Crowther gives the following thought-provoking account of the purpose for the death of a son of Wilford Woodruff:

---

26. Dyer, *Who Am I?*, p. 489.

27. Bruce R. McConkie, *Mormon Doctrine* (Salt Lake City: Bookcraft, Inc., 1966), p. 762.

Wilford Woodruff learned by revelation that his son, Brigham, who drowned in northern Utah, had been called to labor for his relatives beyond the veil: . . . About this time, one of his choicest and most spiritual-minded sons, Brigham Y. Woodruff was drowned in Bear River, in Cache Valley. President Woodruff, having attached considerable importance to the future of this noble son, was very much grieved because of his death. Although he never murmured at the providences of the Almighty, he inquired of the Lord to know why it should be thus. The Lord revealed to him that as he was doing such an extensive work in the Temples for the dead, his son Brigham was needed in the spirit world to preach the gospel and labor among those relatives there."[28]

What peace it brings me to have some idea of where Stephen's spirit is now and what he is doing. In the words of Heber J. Grant:

I never think of my wives and my dear mother, my two boys, my daughter, my departed friends, and my beloved associates as being in the graveyard. . . . My mind reaches out to the wonderful joy and satisfaction and happiness that they are having, and it robs the grave of its sting.[29]

Why Is the Resurrection Important?

As I learned something about the spirit world—how wonderful it is and how happy and active Stephen's life is there—I remember well wondering in my heart why the resurrection from the dead is so important if life in the spirit world is so good.

---

28. Duane S. Crowther, *Life Everlasting* (Salt Lake City: Bookcraft, Inc., 1971), p. 205. See entire book for in-depth treatment of life after death.

29. Bryant S. Hinckley, *Heber J. Grant, Highlights in the Life of a Great Leader* (Salt Lake City: Deseret Book Co., 1951), pp. 248-49.

Upon further investigation, however, I learned that life as a spirit, wonderful though it may be, is a limited way of life. In the words of Joseph F. Smith:

> . . . when we put on immortality, our condition will be very different, for we ascend into an enlarged sphere; although we shall not become perfect immediately after our departure from the body, for the spirit without the body is not perfect, and the body without the spirit is dead. The disembodied spirit during the interval of the death of the body and its resurrection from the grave is not perfect, hence it is not prepared to enter into the exaltation of the celestial kingdom; but it has the privilege of soaring in the midst of immortal beings, and of enjoying, to a certain extent, the fullness of the reward which we are seeking and which we are destined to receive if found faithful to the law of the celestial kingdom, but only in part.[30]

Time spent in the spirit world, therefore, is only a waiting period between the mortal state and the resurrected state. "After all men are resurrected, the spirit world will be without inhabitants."[31] In the Book of Alma we read:

> Now, there is a death which is called a temporal death; and the death of Christ shall loose the bands of this temporal death, that all shall be raised from this temporal death.
>
> The spirit and the body shall be reunited again in its perfect form; both limb and joint shall be restored to its proper frame, even as we now are at this time.[32]

In the words of Mark E. Petersen:

> Matthew records that following the resurrection of the Savior, many others who had died came forth from their graves and appeared to those in the city. But the sacred record tells us

---

30. JD, XIX, 260-61, 264.
31. McConkie, *Mormon Doctrine*, p. 762.
32. Alma 11:42-43.

that each one of us also shall be resurrected in as real a manner as was the Savior.

Each bone shall return to its proper place, flesh and sinews shall come upon them, all shall be restored to the proper and perfect frame. Humanity shall be brought forth from the grave, not as spirits, but as physical beings who can eat as did Jesus, who can be felt as Jesus, and who can appear to other people as He did.

Alma, in his fortieth chapter, comforts all men with the assurance that as the body comes forth it shall be in perfect condition, and that not so much as a hair of the head will be lost. All will be restored to a perfect condition. The resurrection will be universal. As in Adam all die, even so in Christ shall all be made alive, taught the Apostle Paul.[33]

The love of George Albert Smith for all mankind is apparent in these words:

I wish that all the people of the world—all our Father's children—could understand the scriptures that have been given to us by the Lord and preserved by his servants. They are replete with assurance of the resurrection and eternal life.[34]

Man needs his body, as well as his spirit, if he is to have a fullness of joy and continue along the path towards exaltation. Lorenzo Snow tells us:

Nothing is so beautiful as a person in a resurrected and glorified condition. There is nothing more lovely than to be in this condition and have our wives and children and friends with us.[35]

---

33. Mark E. Petersen, "The Resurrection Is Real," *Patterns for Living* (Salt Lake City: Bookcraft, Inc., 1962), p. 277.

34. Burton and Burton, *For They Shall Be Comforted,* p. 95.

35. *Ibid.,* pp. 95-96.

My soul rejoices in this understanding which brings a deep appreciation for Jesus Christ and His sacrifice for us which overcame both physical and spiritual death.

Children Who Die Will Develop After Resurrection

But what of the resurrection of little children whose physical bodies never developed to adult stature in mortality? Will they ever have the opportunity of growing as they would have had they lived to maturity? On several occasions the Prophet Joseph Smith made statements in funeral addresses concerning the resurrection of little children and their future physical development. Some question arose as to the Prophet's exact meaning in these statements. B. H. Roberts and Joseph F. Smith both interviewed persons who were present at the funerals in question and clarified this doctrine.[36] In the *Improvement Era* in June, 1904, Joseph F. Smith made the following statement:

> The body will come forth as it is laid to rest, for there is no growth or development in the grave. As it is laid down, so will it rise, and changes to perfection will come by the law of restitution. But the spirit will continue to expand and develop, and the body, after the resurrection will develop to the full stature of man.[37]

And in *Gospel Doctrine* he records:

> Joseph Smith declared that the mother who laid down her little child, being deprived of the privilege, the joy, and the

---

36. See also HC, IV, 556-57 (March 20, 1842); HC, VI, 316 (April 7, 1844); Smith, *Gospel Doctrine,* pp. 455-57; Wilford Woodruff, JD, XVIII, 32.

37. Joseph F. Smith, "On the Resurrection," *Improvement Era,* VII (June, 1904), 623-24.

satisfaction of bringing it up to manhood or womanhood in this world, would, after the resurrection, have all the joy, satisfaction, and pleasure, and even more than it would have been possible to have had in mortality, in seeing her child grow to the full measure of the stature of its spirit. . . . When she does it there, it will be with the certain knowledge that the results will be without failure; whereas here the results are unknown until after we have passed the test.[38]

I have particularly appreciated the statement of Sister M. Isabella Horne on this subject:

> In conversation with the Prophet Joseph Smith once in Nauvoo, the subject of children in the resurrection was broached. I believe it was in Sister Leonora Cannon Taylor's house. She had just lost one of her children, and I had also lost one previously. The Prophet wanted to comfort us, and he told us that we should receive those children in the morning of the resurrection just as we laid them down, in purity and innocence, and we should nourish and care for them as their mothers. He said that children would be raised in the resurrection just as they were laid down, and that they would obtain all the intelligence necessary to occupy thrones, principalities and powers. The idea that I got from what he said was that the children would grow and develop in the Millennium, and that the mothers would have the pleasure of training and caring for them, which they had been deprived of in this life.[39]

Oh, what a blessing it is to have such knowledge available to us! How often I have stood at the side of Stephen's grave and looked forward to that marvelous day of resurrection. I have an abiding hope that the time will come when I will stand at that very spot, where I have stood so often in sorrow, and with joy unspeakable receive my dear baby into my arms again—to nurture, to care for, to love.

---

38. Smith, *Gospel Doctrine,* pp. 453-54.
39. HC, IV, 556-57.

I know that there is only one person who can prevent me from the realization of that hope and that is I myself. Stephen's celestial resurrection is assured. Mine depends upon my righteousness. "Jesus Savior, pilot me . . ."[40] In the words of Joseph Fielding Smith:

> If parents are righteous, they will have their children after the resurrection. Little children who die, whose parents are not worthy of an exaltation, will be adopted into the families of those who are worthy.[41]

What a motivation this realization gives me to strive to live the gospel! Stephen's death and my deep desire to have him in the resurrection, rather than to have someone else raise him, may some day prove to be the greatest possible blessing the Lord could have given me.

Children Who Die May Obtain Exaltation

To inherit the celestial kingdom, which I learned would automatically be Stephen's privilege because he died before he became accountable, surely is a wonderful blessing. But would he ever be able to obtain exaltation in that kingdom and what would be necessary for him to do so? LeGrand Richards defines what exaltation consists of:

> Men can become Gods and enjoy a "fullness and a continuation of the seeds forever and ever," only by observing the new and everlasting covenant of marriage, and . . . without marriage they can only become "ministering servants, to minister for those who are worthy of a far more, and an exceeding, and an eternal weight of glory."[42]

---

40. *Hymns of The Church of Jesus Christ of Latter-day Saints,* (Salt Lake City: The Church, 1965), p. 121.

41. Smith, *Doctrines of Salvation,* II, 56.

42. LeGrand Richards, *A Marvelous Work and a Wonder* (Salt Lake City: Deseret Book Co., 1950), p. 263.

and in the words of Lynn McKinlay:

> In the Doctrine and Covenants 131:1-4, we are informed that celestial marriage is essential to the obtaining of the highest degree of glory in the celestial kingdom.[43]

Joseph Fielding Smith explains what is necessary for children to obtain exaltation:

> Little children who die before they reach the years of accountability will automatically inherit the celestial kingdom, but not the exaltation in that kingdom until they have complied with all the requirements of exaltation. For instance:
>
> The crowning glory is marriage and this ordinance would have to be performed in their behalf before they could inherit the fullness of that kingdom. The Lord is just with all his children, and little children who die will not be penalized . . . simply because they happen to die. The Lord will grant unto these children the privilege of all the sealing blessings which pertain to the exaltation.[44]

Since Stephen was not able to be married, and the sealing of marriage is an ordinance which must be performed prior to the resurrection,[45] this work will have to be done for him by proxy. Is there some work we need do for him now? In *Doctrines of Salvation* we read:

> All that we need do for children is to have them sealed to their parents. They need no baptism and never will, for our Lord has performed all the work necessary for them . . .
>
> Boys and girls who die after baptism may have the endowment work done for them in the temple. Children who die in infancy do not have to be endowed. So far as the ordinance of sealing [marriage] is concerned, this may wait until the millennium.[46]

---

43. Lynn A. McKinlay, *Life Eternal* (Salt Lake City: Deseret Book Co., 1954), p. 91.

44. Smith, *Doctrines of Salvation,* II, 54-55.

45. Talmage, *Jesus the Christ,* p. 548.

46. Smith, *Doctrines of Salvation,* II, 54-55.

Melvin J. Ballard once lost a child and received for himself the following spiritual assurance in relation to this question of exaltation:

> Yes, even though some mortals die in infancy, that is no loss; no child has lost anything, for all the experiences that he would have had, had he lived, are only postponed. It will all come to them. I know when we lost a little boy some six years of age I grieved over it, because I thought in my very sadness that he had lost something great. I grieved over it, and I thought, is it possible because of his death that he never will have the privilege of gaining that great exaltation? And the Lord whispered peace to my soul and gave me a revelation for myself—not a revelation for the Church, but just a revelation for my peace and comfort—that in the Lord's own time my son will have every right to choose a companion and receive the sealing powers that will unite him with one of his own choosing so that he can pass by the gods unto his own exaltation. When the right time comes the Lord will reveal it.[47]

How marvelous it is to realize that a way has been provided whereby Stephen will be entitled to all the blessings he would have received had he remained here long enough to obtain them.

After Stephen's passing, I had a real struggle trying to accept Stephen's death with the same peace in my subconscious as I did in my conscious mind. I suppressed my grief and it manifested itself in physical illness. My mind said aloud that it was all right that Heavenly Father called Stephen into the spirit world, but my subconscious grieved and mourned. Time and again deep emotion would well up out of me, when I thought it was all under control.

On November 17, 1972 our sixth child, Christian Vassel, was born. Even as I came to the hour of travail, I wept for

47. Ballard, *Crusader for Righteousness,* p. 278.

Stephen and feared the child about to be born would also die. I had fasted and prayed for the Spirit of our Lord and Savior to be my constant companion during the hours of birth. Surely the Lord heard my yearnings, and blessed me with a gift far beyond my expectations and hopes.

Shortly after Christian's birth, I was taken into the recovery room and left alone to rest and be observed periodically, according to standard hospital procedure. Shortly after the nurse left me, I suddenly had an overwhelmingly strong feeling that someone was standing by my head and to the left of me. The feeling was so powerful I turned on the bed, as best I could, to look behind me. All that I saw was the dim corner of the room. Then a wonderful feeling of joy welled up in me, and into my mind came the thought, "Stephen's here!"

I looked away, and again the feeling that someone was standing at my left, a little behind me, was so powerful that once more I turned to look. I saw Stephen, not with my physical eyes, but in a manner very real to me. He was an adult young man, and on his face was a sublime expression of love for me and of compassion and sympathy. Then his words came clearly to my mind. They were exact and indelible in their impression: "Well, Mother, now you have your baby, and there's no more need to grieve for me. We'll have our time in the resurrection, and now I'm free to do my work in the spirit world." I turned to look a third time, but Stephen was gone.

Exactly how I saw him is difficult to put into words because such sight is not within our usual experience. But usual or not, it was very very real. He was adult in stature, and dressed in white. My impression is that the material he wore was softly draped, but I can't describe his clothing in any detail. His height was about that of my husband, but his frame was larger. His hair was sandy colored with a soft wave in it, and his jaw square and muscular.

How gracious and loving our Father in Heaven is to us! Those words were exactly what I needed, for my particular situation. I had feared to yield my love to another baby because I did not want to neglect and forget Stephen, but Stephen encouraged me not to be afraid to love Christian with all my heart, for Stephen and I would have our time together, and somehow my grief prevented him from being truly free to do his work in the spirit world. The change that communication made in me and my feelings was as distinct as the difference between night and day. I have loved and savored every precious moment of every day with Christian, and because of that message from Stephen I now feel completely free to do so. How grateful I am for the gospel of Jesus Christ and for answers to prayers which satisfy so beautifully one's personal needs.

CHAPTER 4

RETARDED CHILDREN

In the course of my search for information and understanding concerning Heavenly Father's plan for little children who die, I have read statements to the effect that "every principle governing the salvation of little children applies with equal force to persons of any age who do not arrive at the years of accountability."[1]

On the surface, it appears that there has not been a great deal written in the scriptures and by Church leaders dealing specifically with retarded children. However, the volume of such writings becomes much larger when one realizes that all that has been said about little children who die before becoming accountable applies with equal weight to those who are mentally retarded. "In the hope of casting a ray of comfort through the cloud of grief. . ."[2] that overshadows many who have been tried in this manner, let us examine a few truths which the Lord has made known relating specifically to retarded children.

The Eternal Spirit of a Retarded Child Is Not Affected

The question has been asked whether the eternal spirit of a retarded child is in any way injured by the handicapped condition of the child. Clifford E. Young said in General Conference of the Church in 1954:

1. McConkie, *Mormon Doctrine,* p. 675.

2 [Bennion?], *Liahona—the Elder's Journal,* p. 1227.

I was in the home two weeks ago of one of our brethren where there is a little girl who is deficient, a little child who never will have the opportunity in this life to fulfill the purposes of the Lord for which she was placed here, unless God shall intervene with a miracle and heal her little body and her mind. Her mind apparently through some physical pressure and through no fault of her own, nor is it through any failure of her parents to do the will of the Lord, is not able to grasp the things that you and I are able to grasp, and thus she will go through life underprivileged, not physically only, but lacking in the expression of her mental powers. It is not her spirit that is injured, but her body, and the body is the medium of expression of the spirit in this life; and when the body is injured either in birth or before or afterwards, and as a result the spirit cannot give expression to a normal life here, then we speak of such as being defective, and handicapped.[3]

Consider also the words of Joseph Fielding Smith:

We do not expect mentally deficient children to remain so after the resurrection; the condition under which they suffer now is one that pertains to the mortal condition, with all its defects and restrictions.[4]

We may feel assured that when a mentally retarded person leaves this mortal sphere, he will have all the mental powers that his brothers and sisters do. "How grateful Latter-day Saints should be that the truth has been restored. The spirit of every child born into this world was mature in the pre-existence. We lived in the presence of our Eternal Father. We were taught his laws and obeyed them. We had knowledge and understanding far beyond anything we gain in this life. Naturally, that which we gained by obedience in

3. CR (April 5, 1954), p. 94.
4. Smith, *Doctrines of Salvation,* II, 55-56.

the pre-existence will in the next world be restored to us.[5] Joseph F. Smith said concerning this matter:

> Every spirit that comes to this earth to take upon it a tabernacle is a son or a daughter of God, and possesses all the intelligence and all the attributes that any son or daughter can enjoy.[6]

Why Are Some Persons Mentally Retarded?

But why, then, are some children mentally retarded for the span of this life? Some have suggested that these children may be sent here to this earth to provide a test for others, rather than to be tested themselves. This may well be true. In reading section twenty-nine of the Doctrine and Covenants, wherein the Lord says that Satan is not given power to tempt little children and "he that hath no understanding,"[7] one is struck by verse 48:

> For it is given unto them [little children and he that hath no understanding] even as I will, according to mine own pleasure, that great things may be required at the hand of their fathers.

The opportunity of having a special child in one's home often does require great things of the parents. He who sends us great trials also will send us great blessings if we will but look unto Him. These experiences provide us with real incentive to ask for comfort, for answers, for strength. Someday we may well find that these trials are in reality among the greatest possible of blessings, though now they appear to us as blessings in disguise.

---

5. Smith, *Improvement Era,* LIX, p. 703.

6. Smith, *Gospel Doctrine,* p. 453.

7. D&C 29:46-50.

The Eternal Plan for Retarded Children

What is the plan that Heavenly Father has for retarded children, and what do we know of their eternal opportunities? As mentioned previously, the scriptures class these people among those who are redeemed as little children. In the book of Moroni we read: "For behold that all little children are alive in Christ, and also "they that are without the law."[8] The Gospel teachings give us divine law, and a commandment to obey or forfeit eternal blessings. This plan is based upon the premise that we can understand these laws and intelligently exercise our free choice as to whether or not we will conform our lives to them. When we have the capacity to understand, we are then accountable when eight years old.[9] But what of children who do not develop mentally to the age of accountability? In the words of Bruce R. McConkie:

> Obviously if children or adults do not develop mentally to the point where they know right from wrong and have the normal intellect of an accountable person, they never arrive at the years of accountability no matter how many actual years they may live. Such persons, though they may be adults, are without the law, cannot repent, are under no condemnation.[10]

Such children are pure before the Lord, and have no need for baptism, no matter what their age. They are saved in the celestial kingdom[11] and will never be subject to the temptations of Satan.[12] Such persons may, of course, be sealed to their parents, but no other ordinance is necessary for them at the present time.

---

8. Moroni 8:22.

9. D&C 68:27.

10. McConkie, *Mormon Doctrine,* p. 853.

11. HC, 11, 381.

12. See pages 37-38 for an explanation of this doctrine.

Concerning the future of retarded children beyond this life, Clifford E. Young tells us:

> For those who are mentally deficient, through no fault of their own, someday these pressures will be lifted. The healing power of the Almighty will come to their bodies, just as it will come to ours, and as it came to the body of the Savior; and their spirits, which are the offspring of God, will have the privilege of inhabiting bodies, their own bodies that will be healed and free from pressures and afflictions so that there will be no limit to the possibilities of their spirits, their minds, and their souls.[13]

What joy this promise brings! Not only will they inherit the celestial kingdom, but they may also go forward to exaltation in the highest of three heavens within the celestial kingdom if they so desire. The necessary ordinance of marriage for such an exaltation will be performed for them during the millennium.[14]

We go to the temples of the Lord and perform ordinances necessary for the exaltation of our ancestors who lived on the earth at a time when the laws and ordinances of exaltation were not available to them. They lived without gospel law and shall be judged without that law concerning their earthly conduct. Likewise, it should not seem strange to us that the Lord has a plan for retarded children, who "live without law," in this mortal sphere, to also reach the heights. Clifford E. Young tells us:

> The Lord has said that those who live without law shall be judged without law, and by the same token those who are not privileged to have the blessings in this life that you and I have who are mentally and physically able and strong, they also shall ultimately receive blessings from our heavenly Father, and

---

13. CR (April 5, 1954), p. 95.

14. See pages 50-52 for an explanation of this doctrine.

through the atonement of Jesus Christ, blessings that are withheld from them through no fault of their own shall not be withheld from them.[15]

Having such a child truly becomes a sacred trust. The difference between successfully rising to the challenge and being overwhelmed by it depends upon a subtle combination of arming oneself with knowledge and with the spirit of the Lord. We must accept that "into each life some rain must fall." If the rain be the burden of a retarded child, and we successfully meet the challenge, from that day forward we develop empathy, understanding and compassion. We find ourselves being led farther along the road to becoming like the Savior. In the words of Elder Young:

> May the Lord help us to understand these things better than we have in the past, and may he give comfort to the hundreds and thousands of mothers whose hearts are bleeding because of the deficiencies in their children, deficiencies that have come through no fault of the parents and no fault of the child.[16]

Despite the heartache and the turmoil, we may learn lessons that can be taught in no other way.

---

15. CR (April 5, 1954), p. 95.
16. *Ibid.*

CHAPTER 5

OVERCOMING THE CHALLENGE

One might compare the experience of facing a tragedy to falling into a turbulent river full of rapids and boulders. At first there is no fighting the flood, and one can only be swept along by the rushing torrent, using all available strength just to keep one's head above water. Then, gradually, a person begins to get his bearings and can hold onto a rock here, another there, each time getting a firmer and firmer grip. Finally you are able to grasp onto a log which carries you to quieter waters, and with the passage of time to reach the shore and climb out onto the bank. The rushing river will always be there to look upon with reflection and reverence. Rich are the memories of the struggles fought therein, and the lessons learned can often be applied again later in life. Overcoming the torrent is accomplished by a combination of faith in and study of gospel truth, praying unceasingly, the passage of time, and the maintaining of a positive attitude.

The Necessity of a Positive Attitude

There are some who accept the teachings of the restoration but have been puzzled as to why they still feel so overwhelmed by a tragedy. Stephen R. Covey aptly points out that, "All problems ultimately are spiritual . . ." and then goes on to say, "Your problems begin first in your own heart. 'Keep thy heart with all diligence; for out of it are the issues of life.' "[1] No

---

1. Stephen R. Covey, *Spiritual Roots of Human Relations* (Salt Lake City: Deseret Book Co., 1970), p. 282. The passage cited is Proverbs 4:23.

matter how much you believe the principles of the gospel, if your attitude is basically a negative one, you dam yourself off from the powers of heaven which bring one the strength to overcome whatever trial life may bring. President McKay says:

> Contentment springs from within ourselves. It springs from our thoughts. Outward circumstances will be contributive to it, but it is our attitude toward those exterior things which will determine our contentment . . .[2]

A mother of several children gave birth to a retarded child, and from the time she first saw her baby something inside her held back and she had a very difficult time truly accepting the child. As time went by, her attitude was reflected in their home and in the attitude of the other children towards the little one. She knew something was terribly wrong, and was heartbroken to see the effects of the family attitude growing. Yet she did not know how to change her feelings.

One fast Sunday she heard another sister who also had a retarded child bear testimony of her gratitude for her child and the sweet effect the child had upon their home. The first mother later visited the second, and together they attempted to understand the reason for the difference in their two situations. Following this visit, the first mother humbly sought the Lord for the gift of true love for her child. She made every effort to think in a positive manner about her retarded child, and to act as if she had these virtues already, which is faith in action. Gradually, she learned to express gratitude to the Lord for her child. Later, she returned to the second sister and shed humble tears as she told of the beautiful change not only in her own feelings but in those of every other member of her family. In the words of Stephen R. Covey:

---

2. David O. McKay, *Pathways to Happiness* (Salt Lake City: Bookcraft, Inc., 1961), p. 292.

The accomplishing power of a positive mind is unbelievably great. It is like the mind of the Lord, the great Creator. The evil one inspires negative thinking and defeatism. Just as faith without works is dead, so also is works without faith.[3]

Acting "as if" one already has virtues and abilities one earnestly desires is a true principle of power. Concerning this matter, Sterling W. Sill has said:

> The famous "as if" principle of William James might supply us with some good supplementary reading for the Sermon on the Mount. Mr. James said that if you want a quality, act "as if" you already had it. That is, if you want to be friendly, act "as if" you were already friendly. If you want to be courageous, act "as if" you were already courageous. Don't go around imitating cowards or indulging in negative, unchristian thinking. If you want to be faithful, act "as if" you are already faithful. Do the things that faithful people do. Go to church, say your prayers, study the scriptures, be honest with yourself and everyone else. Act "as if" you were a true-blue follower of Christ. Near perfection is very easy once we really get the spirit of it.[4]

In the words of Harold B. Lee:

> Having gone through some similar experiences in losing loved ones in death, I speak from personal experience when I say to you who mourn, do not try to live too many days ahead. The all-important thing is not that tragedies and sorrows come into our lives, but what we do with them. Death of a loved one is the most severe test that you will ever face, and if you can rise above your griefs and if you will trust in God, then you will be able to surmount any other difficulty with which you may be faced.[5]

---

3. Covey, *Spiritual Roots of Human Relations,* pp. 281-82.

4. Sterling W. Sill, *The Law of the Harvest* (Salt Lake City: Bookcraft, Inc., 1963), p. 58.

5. Harold B. Lee, *From the Valley of Despair to the Mountain Peaks of Hope* (Salt Lake City: Deseret News Press, 1971), p. 10. Memorial service address delivered May 30, 1971.

Time and again, as we faced one difficult situation after another with little Stephen, these words of the Lord came to my mind: "Look unto me in every thought; doubt not, fear not."[6] Where there is doubt and fear, there cannot also be the Spirit of the Lord. But as one makes a conscious effort to look unto the Savior in every thought, one is filled with peace.

> These things I have spoken unto you, that in me ye might have peace. In the world ye shall have tribulation: but be of good cheer; I have overcome the world.[7]

Thou Shalt Weep for the Loss of Them That Die

Throughout our whole experience with little Stephen, I have often wondered concerning one's shedding tears when facing deep sorrow. Time and again, tears would well up in me, and either I would force them back, or feel guilty if they did spill over. Is it possible that if one really accepts the Gospel and its teachings, one would have no desire to cry? Such an assumption does not appear to be consistent with the scriptures. In the Doctrine and Covenants the Lord says: "Thou shalt live together in love, insomuch that *thou shalt weep for the loss of them that die,* and more especially for those that have not hope of a glorious resurrection."[8] I am grateful that Stephen does have the promise of a glorious resurrection, and that assurance surely removes from me an added burden. I weep, I suppose, much as a mother does at a missionary farewell. Such a mother knows that what her son or daughter will be doing is a wonderful blessing to all concerned, but the heartstrings are pulled by the separation.[9]

---

6. D&C 6:36.

7. John 16:33.

8. D&C 42:45. Author's italics.

9. Allred, *If A Man Die,* pp, 195-96.

The following thoughts expressed by Lynn McKinlay are truly perceptive concerning this matter:

> Sometimes, as we live out our experiences here we find ourselves in diabolical situations that stretch our reasoning powers almost to the breaking point and harrow our feelings to raw and bleeding wounds. We hardly understand the reasons why certain adversities come to us; we determine to pursue the process of becoming perfect as the scriptures say, then there seems to come an increase of difficulty which tries us to the core. . . . James makes an illuminating comment on the situation.

> My brethren, count it all joy when ye fall into divers temptations'; [In other words let's not become discouraged or bitter or try to justify ourselves in yielding to temptations, but consider trial an opportunity, "count it joy."]

> Knowing this, that the trying of your faith worketh patience.

> But let patience have her perfect work, that ye may be perfect and entire, wanting nothing. (James 1:24)

> Section 101 of the Doctrine and Covenants, gives us the Lord's words in our day on this matter of the value of proving through trial.

> Therefore, they must needs be chastened and tried, even as Abraham, who was commanded to offer up his only son,

> For all those who will not endure chastening, but deny me, cannot be justified. (D&C 101:4-5.)

> In the light of this revealed insight I would not, had I the invitation or the opportunity, go to my fellow men and weep futile tears with them and wail with them against a so-called cruel fate, I am not complimented when someone comes to me and would weep futile tears with me about a sorry plight I may be in and wish I could be spared it all. I believe that God gives us experiences to make us strong, and it is not a compliment when someone, thinking to be kind, would take away from us the very experiences that would make us strong. But this I do believe in: a full, free-flowing flood of sympathy that pours

from heart to heart as oil from vessel to vessel; tears shed with a friend that bring relief, that cleanse, that purify, that we may sustain each other in patience and dignity through the trials of this life, and if we do that we will find the Master standing in our midst.[10]

The Lord did not promise us a life without sorrow even when we have a fullness of the gospel. He said to Eve in the Garden of Eden: ". . . I will greatly multiply thy sorrow and thy conception; in sorrow thou shalt bring forth children."[11]

Jesus Christ, who above all people applied the truths of eternal law in His life, often wept in sorrow for various reasons.[12] Consider the following counsel given in the *Liahona:*

> Is it wrong to weep for those we have lost? No, provided grief is restrained within proper bounds, and does not lead to unbelief nor murmuring against God. . . . It is right to let our tears flow over the dead. Not to shed them would be inhuman; and they relieve the pressure on heart and brain.[13]

How true I know that to be! Brigham Young made the following statement in relation to this question:

> We love to keep together the social family relation that we bear one to another, and do not like to part with each other; but could we have knowledge and see into eternity, if we were perfectly free from the weakness, blindness, and lethargy with which we are clothed in the flesh, we should have no disposition to weep or mourn.[14]

---

10. Lynn A. McKinlay, *For Behold Ye Are Free* (Salt Lake City: Deseret Book Co., 1968), pp. 155-56.

11, Genesis 3:16.

12. John 11:35.

13. [Bennion?], *Liahona—the Elder's Journal,* p. 1229.

14. John A. Widtsoe, (comp.), *Discourses of Brigham Young* (Salt Lake City: Deseret Book Co., 1961), p. 370.

Some have felt this meant we should not weep for our dead, and they quote it to those who face the death of a loved one as much as to say that if one weeps or mourns, there is some doubt as to whether they really believe the gospel. However, upon closer examination of this statement, one can see that Brigham Young did not mean to say that people in this mortal sphere should not weep for their loved ones who die. No man or woman is ever "perfectly free from the weakness, blindness and lethargy" of this mortal life, for as Paul said, "For now we see through a glass, darkly;"[15] and it is intended that in this life man walk by faith rather than by sight. In accordance with Brigham Young's statement, we should strive to seek knowledge and understanding through the Spirit of the Lord, that our grief and weeping not be uncontrolled. But we must not lose sight of the fact that we live in this mortal vale of tears and sorrow. Such tears need not represent a rebellion against the will of the Lord, but only a sorrow at being parted from a dear one. In the words of Gordon T. Allred:

> The word of the Lord in modern times has counseled that, "Thou shalt live together in love, insomuch that thou shalt weep for the loss of them that die. . . ." (D&C 42:45) Therefore, Mormons with all their radiant optimism, do not regard death lightly. Like birth, it is a sacred thing, a matter of profound significance marking the commencement of a new epoch in human advancement. The tears shed are real enough, and why pretend that the passing of a loved one or friend is not the most poignant, the most painful matter of all earthly experience? . . . No, for the most part, the tears that fall do not result from doubt, hopelessness, or the common supposition of the world that dying is the ultimate tragedy, the irretrievable loss. Rather, they evidence the natural feeling of emptiness that accompanies any lengthy separation between people who have dwelt together in intimate faith and love.[16]

---

15. 1 Corinthians 13:12.

16. Allred, *If A Man Die,* p. 195.

The Comforting Assurance of Friends

The comforting assurance of friends can be invaluable at such a time. President David O. McKay captures beautifully this need in the following words:

> I know that for not a few of us the true joy of living is overcast by trials, failures, worries and perplexities. . . . Tear-bedimmed eyes are often blind to the beauties that surround us. Life sometimes seems a parched and barren desert, when, as a matter of fact, there is comfort, even happiness within our grasp if we could or would but reach for it.
>
> Next to a sense of a kinship with God comes the helpfulness, encouragement and inspiration of friends. Friendship is a sacred possession. As air, water and sunshine are to flowers, trees and verdure, so smiles, sympathy and love of friends are to the daily life of man. "To live, laugh, love one's friends, and be loved by them is to bask in the sunshine of life."[17]

Reassurances to a Grieving Mother

One of the greatest sources of comfort to me when Stephen died was an editorial written half-a-century ago in the *Liahona.* Although parts of the editorial answering questions of a mother who had lost three children have already been quoted, it is included now in its entirety (with the exception of the allegory found on pages 26-28 herein) because this article truly qualifies as a classic in Mormon literature.

Why Do Little Children Die?

> . . . Ever since Rachel wept for her children and would not be comforted because they were not; yes, ever since Mother Eve wept in her bitter sorrow, mothers have been asking the questions this one asks. It is not yet given to mortal man to answer them fully. He may not yet make an end entirely of the

---

17. McKay, *Pathways to Happiness,* p. 141.

mystery that surrounds death. The blessing we obtain, or may and ought to obtain, through the death of loved ones, would be lost were a full disclosure of all that pertains to death, made to us in our present state. If by actual sight we could penetrate the veil which separates this world from the next, faith would not be exercised; and without being exercised it could not be developed, and without being developed it could not lay hold on eternal life.

But God in his mercy has not left his Saints wholly without light and knowledge upon this great subject; and in the hope of casting a ray of comfort through the cloud of grief that overwhelms this mother, and of consoling others who have been tried in like manner, we will present a few truths relating to life and death which the Lord has made known.

Why are our little children whom we love so tenderly, taken from us? One reason is to impel us to ask this very question; to fill us with a yearning to know; to draw out our very souls in a search for an explanation. Such a search leads us out of this world into a higher one, and discloses to us truths and principles which we must learn if ever we are saved in the kingdom of God. When one of our little ones is taken from us we are made to realize our helplessness, and that there is One in whose hand is held the power of life and death; and we begin to believe in God more than we did before. Faith in God, the principle by which we are saved, is strengthened.

We leave a world of spirits and enter this one, where we receive our bodies, which, in a little while, we lay in the grave, to enter another spirit world. We will wait and work in that world for a time, until the resurrection, when we will receive our bodies again, and when those of us who are worthy will enter a kingdom of glory. Some of us will receive a glory much greater than that of others, because some will be much more faithful than others. But we are all marching in a vast and resistless procession, and by an overwhelming power we are impelled to pass from one plane of existence to a higher one, a process which always causes pain. We came from the spirit world into this one with a cry of distress, and most of us leave this world and enter the next through the suffering of a death bed.

Why all this pain? Why is the universe filled with it? Because without pain there could not be joy, and "man was created that he might have joy." Sorrow and happiness are opposites, and to know either we must be able to contrast it with the other, in our own experience. Perhaps without knowing it, our sister gives the key to this great mystery—why there is so much pain in the world—in the closing clause of her letter: "We must taste the bitter to know the sweet."

She is troubled to understand why her children were taken, notwithstanding the prayers that were offered up, and the authority of the priesthood that was invoked and exercised, in their behalf. While it is true that God has conferred upon mortal man the priesthood by which, within certain limitations, they have power to act in his name, it is not true that he has conferred upon them the keys of life and death. These keys are held in hands higher than those of mortals. They are used only with a proper regard for the past, the present, and the future; our condition in the spirit world before we came here, our condition here, and our condition in the world to come. Mortal men have not sufficient knowledge of all these conditions to use power over life and death wisely and justly; and therefore this power is, to a great extent, and always in the final issue, withheld from them. By the prayer of faith they can often influence the result, but the decision always rests with God.

The divine promise is that "the prayer of faith shall save the sick;" but in another place this promise is thus qualified: "If they are not appointed unto death." We are thus informed that the sick are sometimes "appointed unto death" by the decree of God; and in such a case even the prayer of faith may be unavailing. But it is not always so. Even the decree of God may possibly be modified in such a case by the prayer of faith. King Hezekiah was sick unto death, and Isaiah, the prophet and mouthpiece of the Lord told him to set his house in order for he should die and not live. But the doomed man prayed the prayer of faith, and the decree that he should die forthwith was modified, and Isaiah told him he should live fifteen years, which he did.

But is it wise to strive to alter our heavenly Father's decree by the prayer of faith? He has great regard for such a prayer; it has great weight with him; and sometimes when we appeal to him in great faith, his love and sympathy for us may move him to grant our petition when a higher wisdom would dictate otherwise. A certain elder in our Church had a little son who was dangerously sick. The father was a man of great faith and refused to give the child up to die, but pleaded with the Lord day and night for his life. The boy recovered, but was a sorrow to his parents from year to year because of his wicked conduct; and many a time they felt that it would have been better, far better, for him and them, had the Lord taken him in his innocence. Other such cases could be cited among the Latter-day Saints, and we are abundantly justified in believing that many little children die in order that they may be preserved from the power and temptations of the adversary.

It is our duty to pray for the sick to be healed, in the manner appointed in the Scriptures, but in praying for this blessing, as for any other, we should do so with this feeling in our hearts: "Thy will and not mine be done." Whether or not the sick are healed, all who take part receive a blessing through praying for them; and they, by this means, obtain a forgiveness of their sins. Such is the promise of the Lord.

The Prophet Joseph once explained that one reason why little children die is that they do not need to remain in this world of sin and sorrow to be prepared for an exaltation in the kingdom of God; and this helps us to understand why "death loves a shining mark," and why our good and bright little ones are so often chosen by the dreaded messenger. President John Taylor once said that the best explanation he could offer why so many little children among the Saints were called away, notwithstanding the great faith and power of the priesthood exercised to keep them here, was that they were bright and noble spirits who held important positions in the kingdom of God in the spirit world, from which they could not long be spared. They were given brief furloughs, long enough to come to earth, take upon themselves bodies of flesh and bone that they might be prepared for a resurrection to a kingdom of glory; and after a short experience in mortality were called back to resume important labors in a higher sphere.

On a certain occasion when a little child lay very sick and in dreadful agony, which was distressing to behold, Apostle Orson Pratt was present, and someone asked, "Why does this little child have to suffer so?" Elder Pratt replied, "It is necessary in order to prepare it for an exaltation." All who live must suffer. It is the law of the universe, resistless and inevitable. He to whom all power was given suffered most of all. In process of time we will learn that relief will come through faith in God, a knowledge of his laws and purposes, and compliance with his will.

This sister wonders if our little ones are taken from us to punish us, and speaks of neglecting to pay tithing. When a mother is weeping over the graves of her children, she needs comfort and consolation rather than rebuke; and the Prophet Joseph once forbade the elders to teach that affliction in the form of sickness and death is always a punishment for sin. So far as the law of tithing is concerned, our heavenly Father will most willingly forgive the past if the law is obeyed in future. But in the hour of trial it is always a comfort to know that we have kept the commandments of the Lord as well as we could.

Is it wrong to weep for those we have lost? No, provided grief is restrained within proper bounds, and does not lead to unbelief nor murmuring against God. The Lord has said:

> Thou shalt live together in love, insomuch that thou shalt weep for the loss of them that die, and more especially for those that have not hope of a glorious resurrection. (D&C 42:45.)

It is right to let our tears flow over the dead. Not to shed them would be inhuman; and they relieve the pressure on heart and brain. Do the dead know of our grief for them? Yes, and if it is uncontrolled it pains them. The mother who wrote the above letter has buried three children. When the second one joined the first behind the veil, what occurred? The new arrival told of matters in the earthly home she had just left. When the third child joined the other two, what happened? The same thing. When our loved ones in this world pass into the next they convey news of us to our loved ones there. . . .

[The allegory cited on pp. 26-28 then follows.]

This mother ought to find a world of comfort in reflecting that she gladly gave bodies to her children with no thought of the cost in pain and danger to herself. In these days of pride and sin, especially secret sin, the angels in heaven honor such a mother, and her reward is sure. She has had it in part in the bright and pure spirits that have been sent to her to be her children; the rest of it will come after she joins those who have gone before.

From reading this mother's letter it is easy for any experienced Latter-day Saint to see that she has already drawn out of her bereavements a great blessing from the Lord; she could not have written such a letter if she had not. Its spirit of earnest inquiry, its intense yearning for more light and satisfaction concerning one of the greatest problems that pertain to mortal existence, and its sweet humility, far more than offset any literary defect, and (make) it not only beautiful but classical. The wisdom the writer seeks will come to her as surely as the sun will continue to shine, if she will but persevere in her search for it; and her soul shall be fully satisfied.

Assuming that this mother will accept the blessings that are within her reach as a Latter-day Saint, she may well take comfort in knowing that, precisely as she laid her little ones in their graves she will receive them in her arms again, when those graves shall be opened at the second coming of Christ. She will have the exquisite happiness of rearing and teaching them, and seeing them grow to maturity in a world that will know no sin nor separation.

She will receive an inheritance in the kingdom of God, and by the side of her husband will sit upon a throne, a queen and goddess, clothed with celestial glory, power and exaltation. Before that throne will stand the children for whose sake she has done and suffered so much; and they and their posterity will love her, and honor her, and pay homage to her forever. She will become a Mother in heaven, and will have power to sympathize with and comfort her children when they pass through what she is passing through now; for they must tread the paths she is now treading, because God's works are one eternal round. God has revealed and promised this unspeakable future to the faithful mothers among his people; and may this one find comfort in the revelations he has given.[18]

After Much Tribulation Come the Blessings

Boyd K. Packer, speaking of the trials faced by many parents, and specifically by mothers, said the following in General Conference:

> I speak a word to mothers who have little children who are handicapped, children whose little bodies were born incompletely formed or whose little minds are limited. No one knows the depth of agony that you have suffered. By way of consolation, I read from the Doctrine and Covenants:
>
> > Ye cannot behold with your natural eyes, for the present time, the design of your God concerning those things which shall come hereafter, and the glory which shall follow after much tribulation.
> >
> > For after much tribulation come the blessings. Wherefore the day cometh that ye shall be crowned with much glory; the hour is not yet, but is nigh at hand. (D&C 58:3-4.)
>
> I . . . suggest that blessings will be extended to mothers such as you who have given tender and affectionate love to handicapped children. Trials such as these bring a reverence for life, a new depth of compassion and motherhood.[19]

Truman Madsen, in his excellent talk, *Power From Abrahamic Tests,* says concerning sacrifice:

> There are sacrifices. But the prophets again and again insist that we ought to use a different word. How can it be called a sacrifice to yield up a handful of dust when what is promised is a whole earth? But we think we know better than God. We think that what we want for us is greater than what he wants for us.

---

18. [Bennion?], *Liahona—the Elder's Journal,* pp. 1226-31.

19. CR (April 5, 1964), p. 85.

Then we simply violate the first commandment, which is to love God first and over all.[20]

In the sixth Lecture on Faith given by the Prophet Joseph Smith, the purpose and result of real personal sacrifice is discussed:

> Let us here observe, that a religion that does not require the sacrifice of all things never has power sufficient to produce the faith necessary unto life and salvation; for, from the first existence of man, the faith necessary unto the enjoyment of life and salvation never could be obtained without the sacrifice of all earthly things. It was through this sacrifice, and this only, that God has ordained that men should enjoy eternal life; and it is through the medium of the sacrifice of all earthly things that men do actually know that they are doing the things that are well pleasing in the sight of God. When a man has offered in sacrifice all that he has for the truth's sake, not even withholding his life, and believing before God that he has been called to make this sacrifice because he seeks to do his will, he does know, most assuredly, that God does and will accept his sacrifice and offering, and that he has not, nor will not seek his face in vain. Under these circumstances, then, he can obtain the faith necessary for him to lay hold on eternal life.
>
> It is in vain for persons to fancy to themselves that they are heirs with those, or can be heirs with them, who have offered their all in sacrifice, and by this means obtain faith in God and favor with him so as to obtain eternal life, unless they, in like manner, offer unto him the same sacrifice, and through that offering obtain the knowledge that they are accepted of him.[21]

Why did this experience come into my life? Is it not possible that it came as a sacred trust? The day before Stephen

---

20. Truman G. Madsen, *Power From Abrahamic Tests* (Provo, Utah: The Brigham Young University Press, 1971), p. 4.

21. N. B. Lundwall, *Discourses on the Holy Ghost* (Salt Lake City: Bookcraft, Inc., 1959), p. 143.

was born, I was a happy mother anticipating the birth of another baby; now I am something more, a different person.

I believe that I have deeper faith in and love for our Father in Heaven and His Son Jesus Christ than ever before. I feel that my soul has been tried in the refiner's fire and has emerged more purified. I know now that my faith is built upon rock, and did not crash around me in the strength of the storm as it would have done had it been built upon sand. I have watched my husband, my children, my parents, my brothers and sisters and my friends all grow in their understanding of the Gospel and the meaning of life and death on this earth since Stephen was born.

Who then can say that little Stephen's illness, his brief life of three-and-a-half months, and his death were useless, meaningless tragedies? I believe with all my heart that his life here was a mission to teach us great truths, a sacred trust for us to cherish and share with others.

BIBLIOGRAPHY

Allred, Gordon T. *If A Man Die.* Salt Lake City: Bookcraft, Inc., 1964.

Andrus, Hyrum L. *God, Man, and the Universe.* Salt Lake City: Bookcraft, Inc., 1968.

Ballard, Melvin R. (comp.). *Melvin J. Ballard. . . Crusader for Righteousness.* Salt Lake City: Bookcraft, Inc., 1967.

(Bennion, Samuel O. ?). "Why Do Little Children Die?," *Liahona—the Elder's Journal,* VI, No. 51 (June 5, 1909), 1226-31.

Brooks, Melvin R. *L.D.S. Reference Encyclopedia.* Salt Lake City: Bookcraft, Inc., 1960.

Burton, Alma and Clea. *For They Shall Be Comforted.* Salt Lake City: Deseret Book Co., 1970.

Burton, Alma Pexton. *Understanding the Things of God.* Salt Lake City: Deseret Book Co., 1966.

Clark, James R. *Messages of the First Presidency.* 5 vols. Salt Lake City: Bookcraft, Inc., 1965.

Clark, J. Reuben. "Man—God's Greatest Miracle." Address given at the summer religious course for seminary and institute teachers at Brigham Young University, June 21, 1954. Provo, Utah: BYU Extension Division, 1954.

Covey, Stephen R. *Spiritual Roots of Human Relations.* Salt Lake City: Deseret Book Co., 1970.

Crowther, Duane S. *Gifts of the Spirit.* Bountiful: Horizon Publishers, 1971.

Crowther, Duane S. *Life Everlasting*. Bountiful: Horizon Publishers, 1971.

Doxey, Roy W. *The Latter-day Prophets and the Doctrine and Covenants*. 4 vols. Salt Lake City: Deseret Book Co., 1963.

Dyer, Alvin Rulon. *Who Am I?* Salt Lake City: Deseret Book Co., 1966.

General Handbook of Instructions. The Church of Jesus Christ of Latter-day Saints. No. 20, 1968.

Hinckley, Bryant S. *Heber J. Grant, Highlights in the Life of a Great Leader*. Salt Lake City: Deseret Book Co., 1951.

Hymns of the Church of Jesus Christ of Latter-day Saints. Salt Lake City: The Church of Jesus Christ of Latter-day Saints, 1965.

Jacob, Carl H. *While of these Emblems*. Salt Lake City: Deseret Book Co., 1962.

Journal of Discourses. 26 vols. Los Angeles: General Printing and Lithograph Co., 1961. Photo lithographic reprint of exact original edition published in 1882. (In this volume cited as JD.)

Kimball, Spencer W. *Tragedy or Destiny*. Address to the Brigham Young University studentbody at Provo, Utah, December 6, 1935. Provo, Utah: BYU Extension Division, 1961.

Lee, Harold B. *From the Valley of Despair to the Mountain Peaks of Hope*. Salt Lake City: Deseret News Press, 1971. Memorial Service address delivered May 30, 1971.

Lundwall, N. B. (comp.). *Discourses on the Holy Ghost*. Salt Lake City: Bookcraft, Inc., 1959.

Madsen, Truman G. *Eternal Man.* Salt Lake City: Deseret Book Co., 1966. See especially "Evil and Suffering."

Madsen, Truman G. *Power from Abrahamic Tests.* Provo, Utah: Brigham Young University Press, 1971.

McConkie, Bruce R. (comp.). *Doctrines of Salvation—Sermons and Writings of Joseph Fielding Smith.* 3 vols. Salt Lake City: Bookcraft, Inc., 1955.

McConkie, Bruce R. *Mormon Doctrine.* 2nd ed. Salt Lake City: Bookcraft, Inc., 1966.

McKay, Llewelyn R. (comp.). *Pathways to Happiness.* David O. McKay. Salt Lake City: Bookcraft, Inc., 1961.

McKinlay, Lynn A. *For Behold Ye Are Free.* Salt Lake City: Deseret Book Co., 1968.

McKinlay, Lynn A. *Life Eternal.* Salt Lake City: Deseret Book Co., 1954.

Official Report of the Annual General Conference of the Church of Jesus Christ of Latter-day Saints. Salt Lake City: The Church of Jesus Christ of Latter-day Saints. (In this volume cited as CR).

Peale, Norman Vincent. *Not Death At All.* New York: Prentice Hall, Inc., 1948.

Petersen, Mark E. *Patterns for Living.* Salt Lake City: Bookcraft, Inc., 1962.

Richards, LeGrand. *A Marvelous Work and a Wonder.* Salt Lake City: Deseret Book Co., 1950.

Rogers, Dale Evans. *Angel Unaware.* Fleming H. Revell Co., 1953.

Romney, George J. (comp.). *Look To God and Live—Discourses of Marion G. Romney.* Salt Lake City: Deseret

Book Co. 1971. See especially "Revelation and How It Comes."

Sill, Sterling W. *The Law of the Harvest*. Salt Lake City: Bookcraft, Inc., 1963.

Smith, Hyrum M. and Sjodahl, Janne M. *The Doctrine and Covenants (Commentary)*. Revised Ed. Salt Lake City: Deseret Book Co., 1957.

Smith, Joseph. *History of the Church of Jesus Christ of Latter-day Saints*. Edited by B. H. Roberts. 7 vols. Salt Lake City: Deseret Book Co., 1959. (In this volume cited as HC).

Smith, Joseph F. *Gospel Doctrine*. Salt Lake City: Deseret Book Co., 1963.

Smith, Joseph Fielding. "Justice For The Dead," *The Ensign*, II, No. 3 (March, 1972), 4.

Smith, Joseph Fielding. "Little Children in the Celestial Kingdom," *Improvement Era*, LIX (October, 1956), 70203.

Smith, Joseph Fielding (comp.). *Teachings of the Prophet Joseph Smith*. Salt Lake City: Deseret Book Co., 1967.

Sperry, Sidney B. *Doctrine and Covenants Compendium*. Salt Lake City: Bookcraft, Inc., 1960.

Talmage, James E. *Jesus The Christ*. Salt Lake City: Deseret Book Co., 1962.

Taylor, John. *Mediation and Atonement of Our Lord and Savior Jesus Christ*. Salt Lake City: Deseret News Co., 1972. Photo lithographic reprint of exact original edition published in 1882.

The Book of Mormon. trans. Joseph Smith. Salt Lake City: The Church of Jesus Christ of Latter-day Saints, 1961.

The Doctrine and Covenants of The Church of Jesus Christ of Latter-day Saints. Salt Lake City: The Church of Jesus Christ of Latter-day Saints, 1961. (In this volume cited as D&C).

The Holy Bible, King James Version; Salt Lake City: The Church of Jesus Christ of Latter-day Saints, 1956.

The Pearl of Great Price. Salt Lake City: The Church of Jesus Christ of Latter-day Saints, 1961.

Widtsoe, John A. (comp.). *Discourses of Brigham Young.* Salt Lake City: Deseret Book Co., 1961.

INDEX

ABOUT THE AUTHOR

Mary Erety Vassel Hill was born in Norwalk, Connecticut in 1941 to Dr. Bruno Vassel and Mary Erety Elmer. At the age of fourteen she went with her family to live in Sao Paulo, Brazil. On board ship going to South America were fourteen Mormon missionaries. Through their influence, Mary became convinced of the truthfulness of the restored Gospel, but her parents forbid her to join the Church. Two years later, after sampling the very sophisticated life of the American colony in Sao Paulo, Mary again turned to the Gospel and as a result of prayer received a burning testimony of its truthfulness. She was baptized November 9, 1972 in a reservoir near the city of Sao Paulo.

While attending Brigham Young University, Mary was her class historian. She also attended Idaho State University and majored in Education.

Since Mary first joined the Church she has been deeply involved in its activities. She participated on the executive committee of the first national Brazilian youth conference and traveled to various cities in Brazil for area conferences. She has been a YWMIA president, a Primary president and counselor, and has also served in a Relief Society presidency. Mary served a mission in Brazil in 1960-61, and also a stake mission in Pocatello, Idaho. She became a Golden Gleaner in 1969.

Mary met her husband, Keith K. Hill, in the Idaho Falls temple and a year later they were married there. Keith is a teacher in the LDS Seminary System. Together they spent two years in Samoa where he taught religion in the Church high school. Mary has traveled extensively in the South Pacific, Europe and South America with her family. They are the parents of six children, and Mary sees her most important church work as that within the sanctuary of her home.